THE BOTTOM OF JAMAICA BAY

# THE BOTTOM OF JAMAICA BAY

## STRUCTURES OF COASTAL RESILIENCE
Jamaica Bay Team
Spitzer School of Architecture
The City College of New York

Catherine Seavitt Nordenson, editor
Associate Professor of Landscape Architecture

Kjirsten Alexander
Research Associate

Danae Alessi
Research Associate

Eli Sands
Research Assistant

# JAMAICA BAY PAMPHLET LIBRARY
01 The Bottom of Jamaica Bay

ISBN 978-1-942900-01-6

## CONTACT
Catherine Seavitt Nordenson
cseavittnordenson@ccny.cuny.edu
www.structuresofcoastalresilience.org

SCR Jamaica Bay Team
The City College of New York
Spitzer School of Architecture
Program in Landscape Architecture, Room 2M24A
141 Convent Avenue New York, New York 10031

## COVER
5 meter resolution bathymetric scale of the Rockaway Inlet from 2011.
source: U.S. National Park Service.

All benthic imagery courtesy of U.S. National Park Service.

supported by

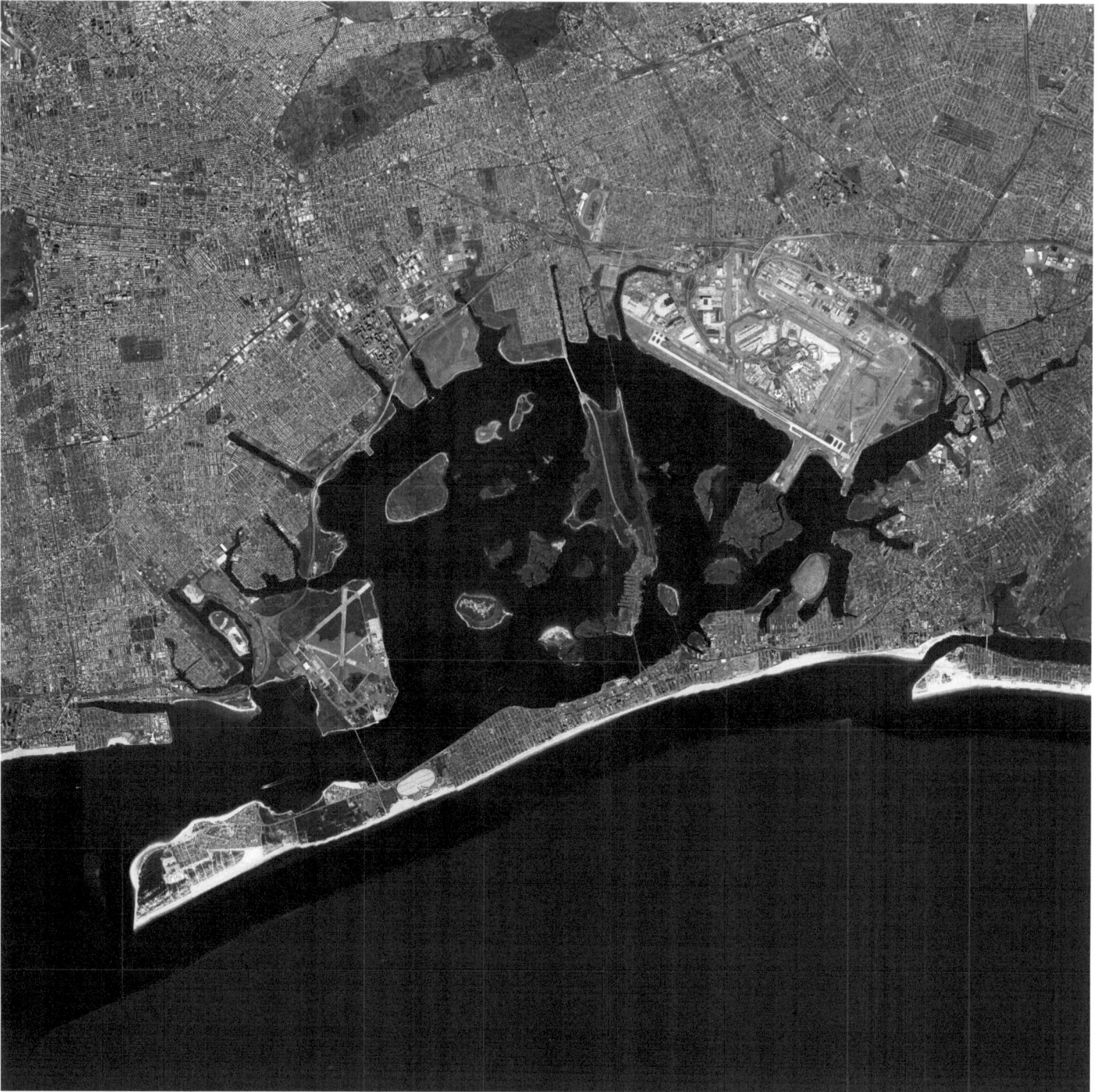

Jamaica Bay aerial

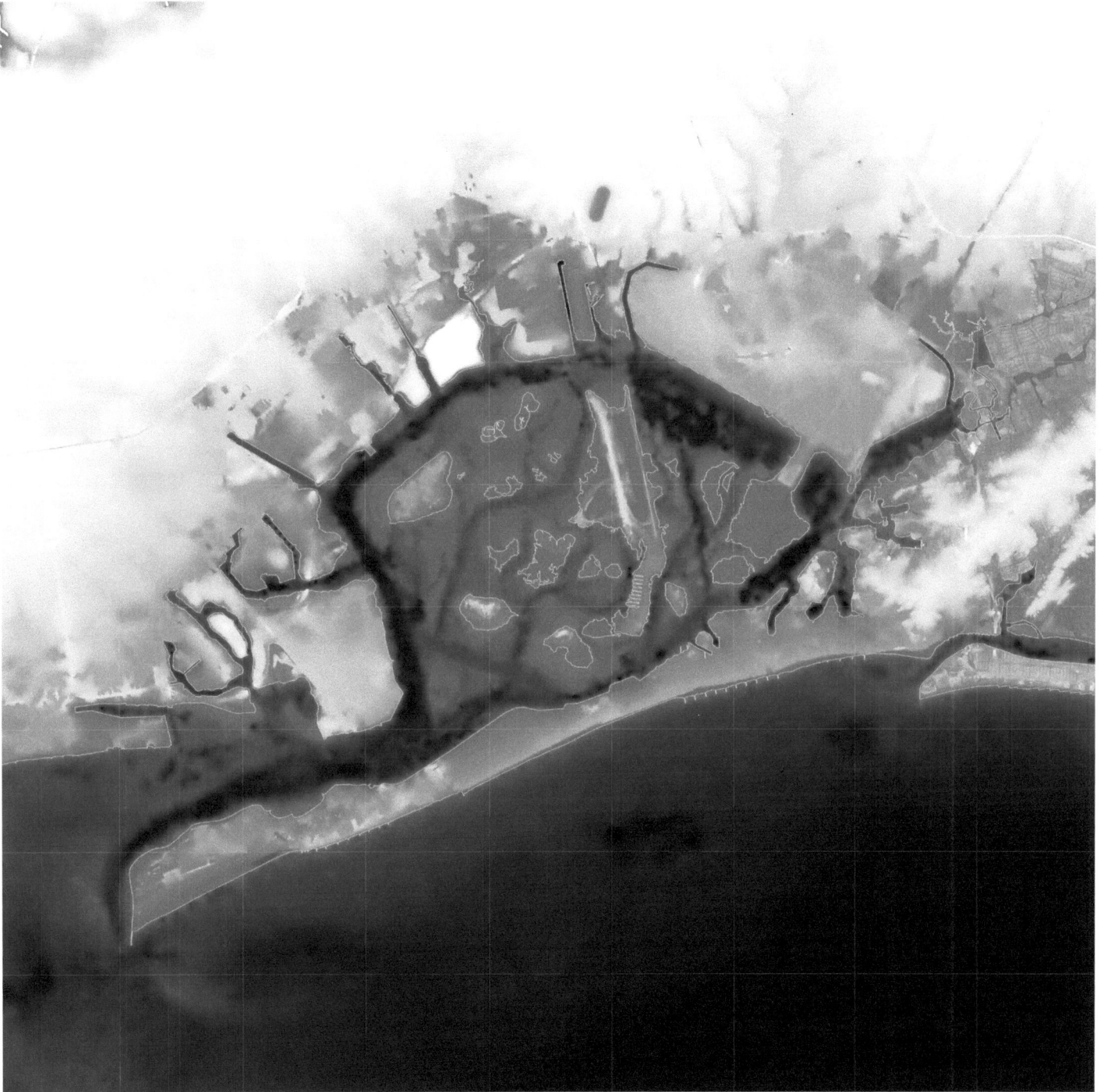

Merged topographic - bathymetric Digital Elevation Model (DEM)

8

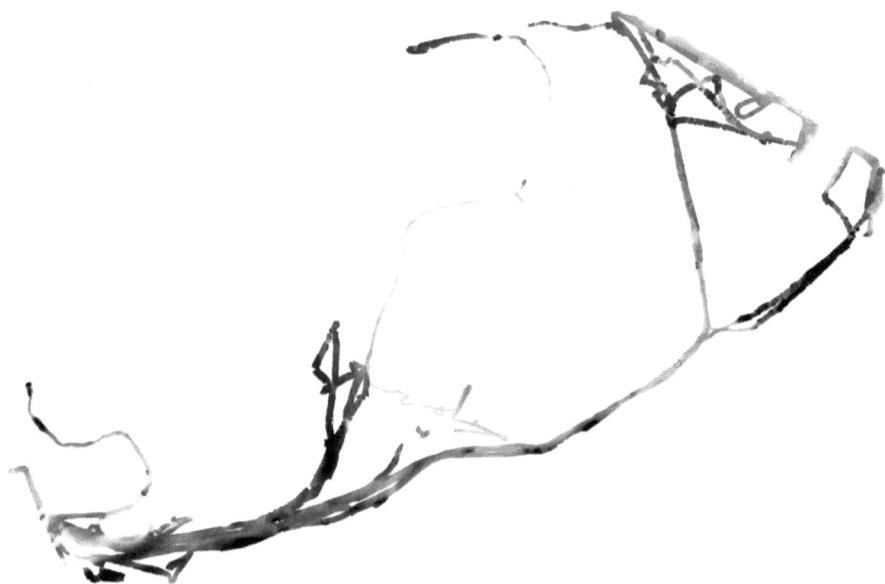

Benthic scans - 1 meter resolution

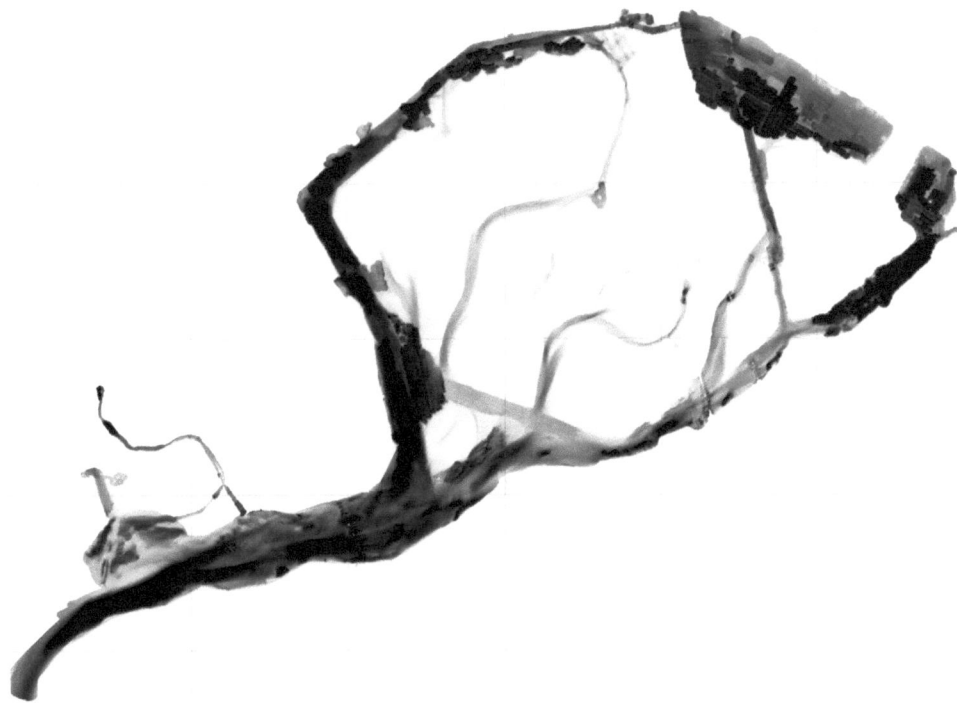

Benthic scans - 5 meter resolution

Rockaway Inlet - 1 meter resolution

Rockaway Inlet - 5 meter resolution

Broad Channel and salt marsh - 1 meter resolution

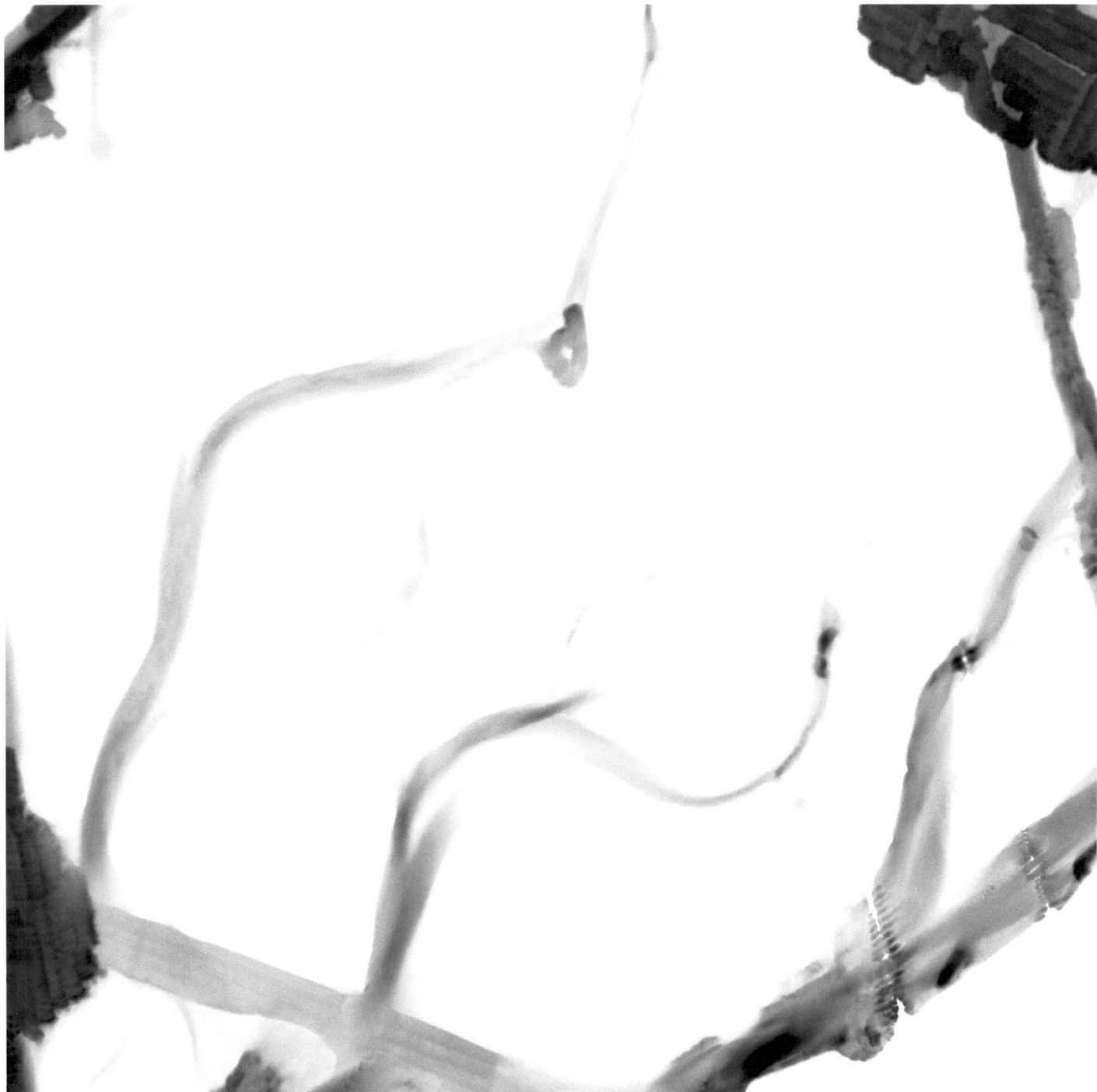

Broad Channel and salt marsh - 5 meter resolution

Grassy Bay - 1 meter resolution

Grassy Bay - 5 meter resolution

-30/b59
-35/b85
-27/b81
-26/b65
-25/b70
-32/b60
-32/b64
-31/b84
-23/b66
-19/b73
-34/b83
-17/b67
-23/b88
-37/b69
-35/b71
-35/b74
-20/b73
-19/b80
-24/b79
-31/b77
-34/b78
-22/b76

-06/b61
-10/b63
-03/b62

-20/b32
-29/b33
-07/b29
-19/b37
-15/b27
-41/b31
-14/b28
-14/b51
-42/b40
-17/b30
-17/b35
-21/b52
-20/b53
-10/b43
-16/b39
-13/b34
-12/b36
-07/b42
-18/b50
-16/b41
-12/b48
-16/b49
-14/b54
-22/b38
-10/b44
-05/b45
-06/b47
-37/b56
-42/b57
-07/b46
-12/b55

-21/b04
-11/b22
-14/b23
-20/b15
-16/b12
-21/b09
-16/b08
-16/b25
-16/b03
-14/b13
-15/b03
-24/b21
-12/b26
-18/b14
-13/b02
-21/b24
-28/b16
-13/b02
-17/b10
-32/b17
-36/b11
-35/b18
-15/b05
-23/b19
-42/b06
-27/b07
-15/b20

-43/b86
-37/b82

18

DEPTH

-14

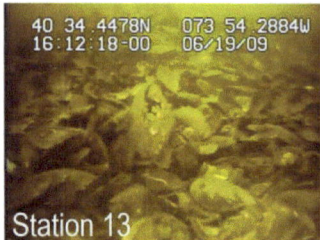

-15

-16

-17

DEPTH

-32

-35

  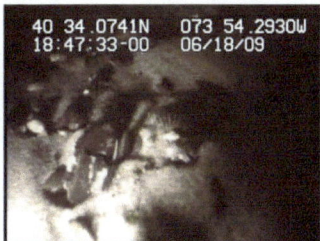 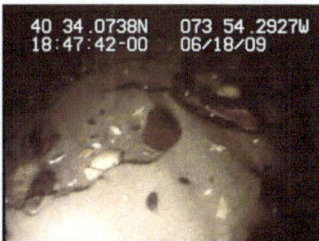

-36

  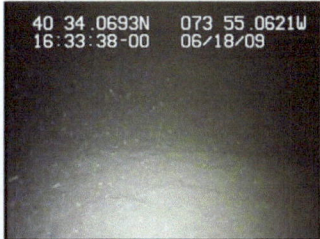 

-42

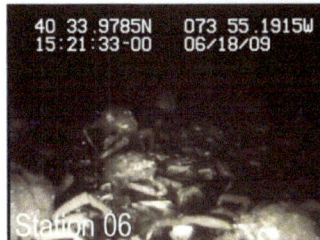 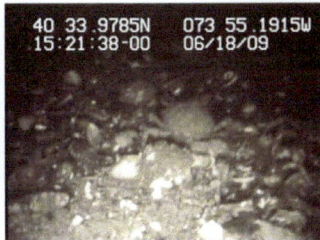 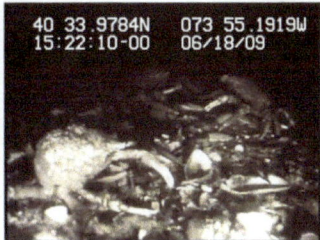 

-30/s59
-32/s60
-32/s84
-35/s85
-27/s81
-31/s64
-26/s65
-25/s70
-19/s72
-22/s66
-17/s67
-23/s68
-34/s83
-37/s69
-35/s71
-35/s74
-20/s73
-19/s80
-24/s79
-31/s77
-34/s78
-22/s76
-06/s61
-10/s63
-03/s62
-20/s32
-29/s33
-07/s29
-19/s37
-41/s31
-14/s28
-15/s27
-14/s51
-42/s40
-17/s30
-21/s52
-20/s53
-17/s35
-13/s34
-10/s43
-16/s39
-07/s42
-16/s41
-12/s36
-18/s50
-12/s48
-18/s49
-05/s45
-14/s54
-32/s56
-22/s38
-10/s44
-06/s47
-12/s55
-07/s46
-42/s57
-37/s58
-43/s86
-37/s82
-21/s04
-11/s22
-21/s09
-14/s23
-20/s15
-16/s12
-16/s25
-16/s08
-14/s13
-16/s03
-15/s03
-18/s14
-28/s16
-13/s02
-13/s02
-24/s21
-12/s26
-21/s24
-17/s10
-32/s17
-36/s11
-35/s18
-13/s05
-23/s19
-42/s06
-27/s07
-15/s20

-05

-06

-07

-10

-12

-13

-14

-15

-16

-17

-18

-19

-20

-21

-22

-29

-32

-37

22

DEPTH

-06

Station 47

-07

 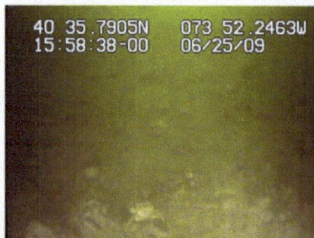 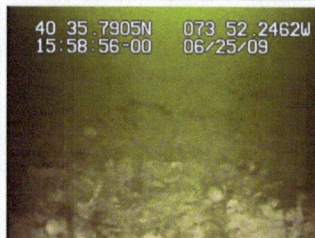 

Stations 29, 42, 46

-10

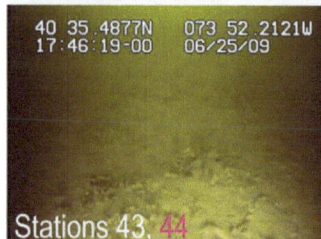 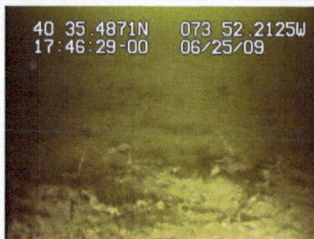 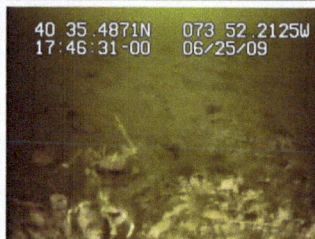 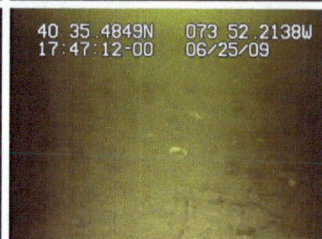

Stations 43, 44

-12

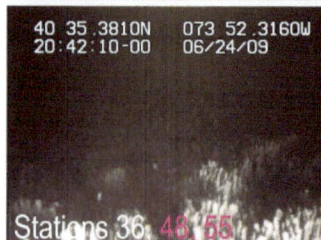 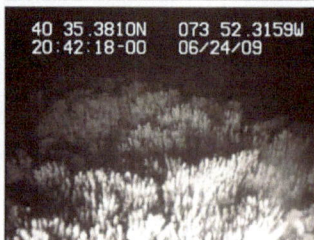 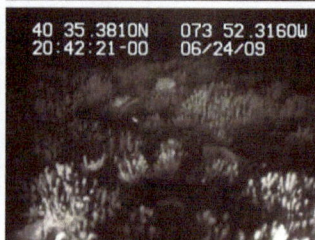 

Stations 36, 48, 55

DEPTH

-21

| | | |
|---|---|---|
| 40 35.5617N 073 51.0184W 16:49:42-00 06/24/09 | 40 35.5617N 073 51.0183W 16:49:46-00 06/24/09 | 40 35.5617N 073 51.0184W 16:49:43-00 06/24/09 | 40 35.5617N 073 51.0183W 16:49:46-00 06/24/09 |

Station 52

-22

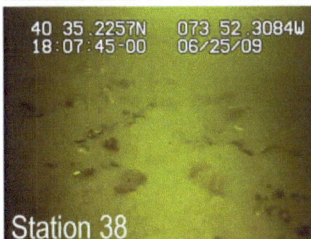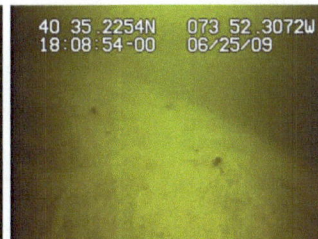

40 35.2257N 073 52.3084W 18:07:45-00 06/25/09

40 35.2255N 073 52.3083W 18:07:58-00 06/25/09

40 35.2255N 073 52.3078W 18:08:25-00 06/25/09

40 35.2254N 073 52.3072W 18:08:54-00 06/25/09

Station 38

-29

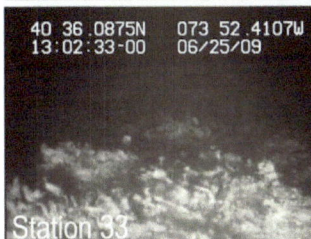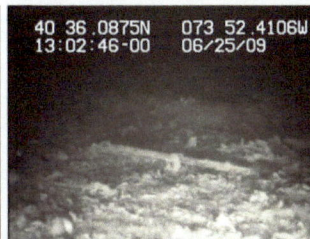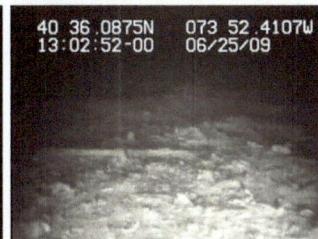

40 36.0875N 073 52.4107W 13:02:33-00 06/25/09

40 36.0875N 073 52.4106W 13:02:43-00 06/25/09

40 36.0875N 073 52.4106W 13:02:46-00 06/25/09

40 36.0875N 073 52.4107W 13:02:52-00 06/25/09

Station 33

-32

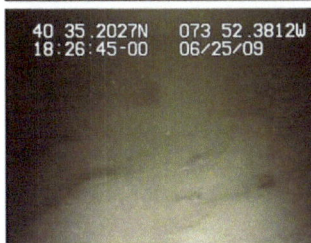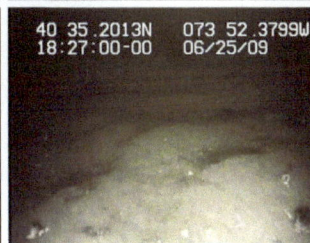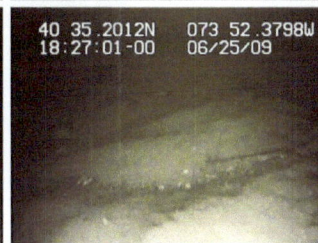

40 35.2027N 073 52.3812W 18:26:45-00 06/25/09

40 35.2016N 073 52.3801W 18:26:57-00 06/25/09

40 35.2013N 073 52.3799W 18:27:00-00 06/25/09

40 35.2012N 073 52.3798W 18:27:01-00 06/25/09

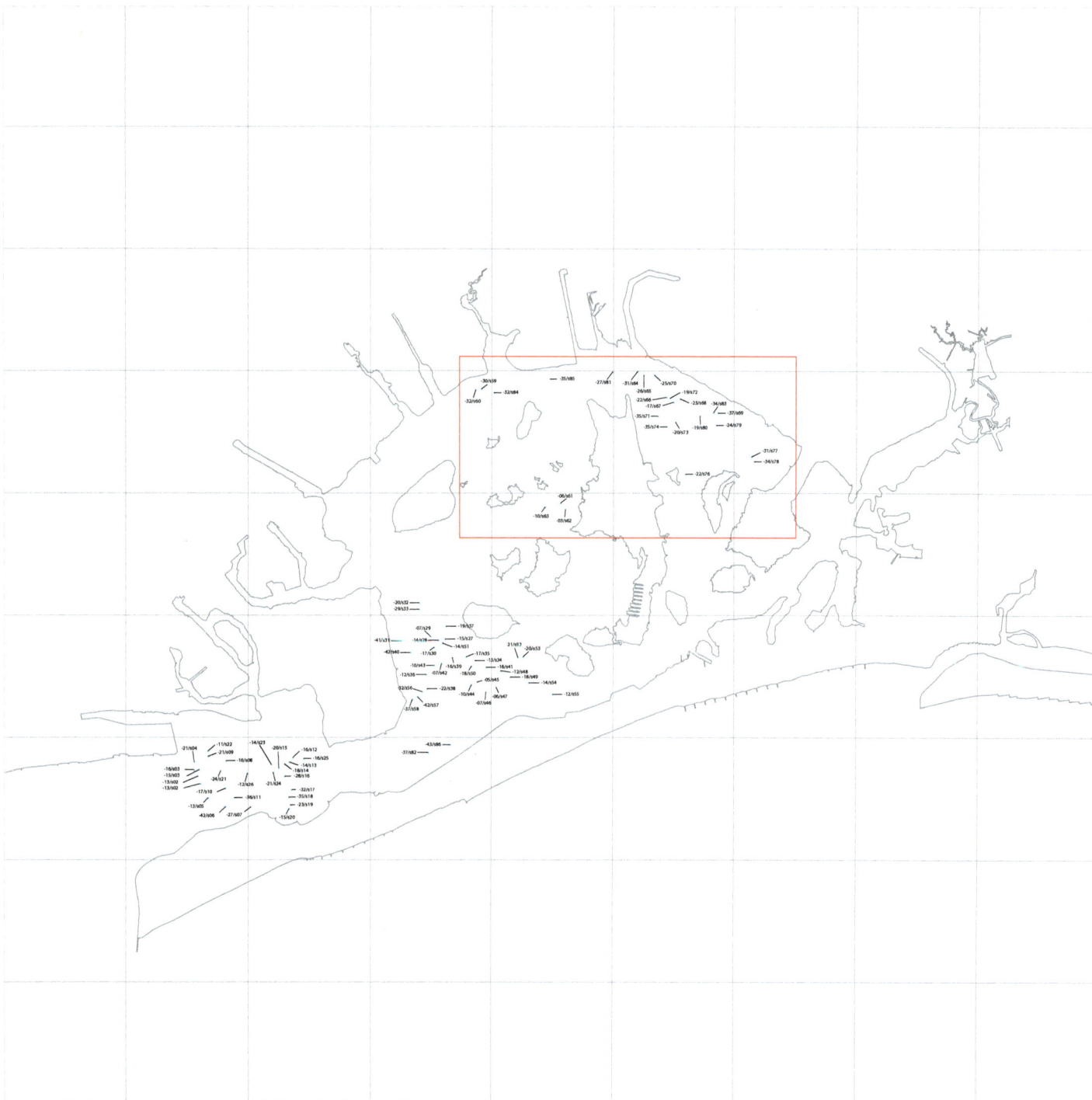

-30/t59  -35/t85  -27/t61  -31/t64  -25/t70
-32/t60  -32/t84  -36/t66  -19/t72
-22/t66  -23/t68  -34/t83
-17/t67  -37/t69
-35/t71
-35/t74  -19/t80  -24/t79
-20/t73

-31/t77
-54/t78

-22/t76

-06/t61
-10/t63
-03/t62

-20/t32
-29/t33

-07/t29
-19/t37
-41/t31  -14/t28  -15/t27
-42/t40  -17/t30  -21/t57  -20/t53
-17/t35
-16/t39  -13/t34
-10/t43  -16/t41
-12/t36  -07/t42  -18/t50  -12/t48  -18/t49  -14/t54
-22/t38  -05/t45
-37/t58  -42/t57  -10/t44  -06/t47  -12/t55
-07/t46

-43/t86
-57/t82

-21/t04  -11/t22  -14/t23  -20/t15  -16/t12
-21/t09  -16/t25
-16/t03  -18/t08  -14/t13
-15/t03  -24/t21  -18/t16
-13/t02  -12/t26  -21/t24
-13/t02  -32/t17
-17/t10  -36/t11  -35/t18
-13/t05  -23/t19
-42/t06  -27/t07  -15/t20

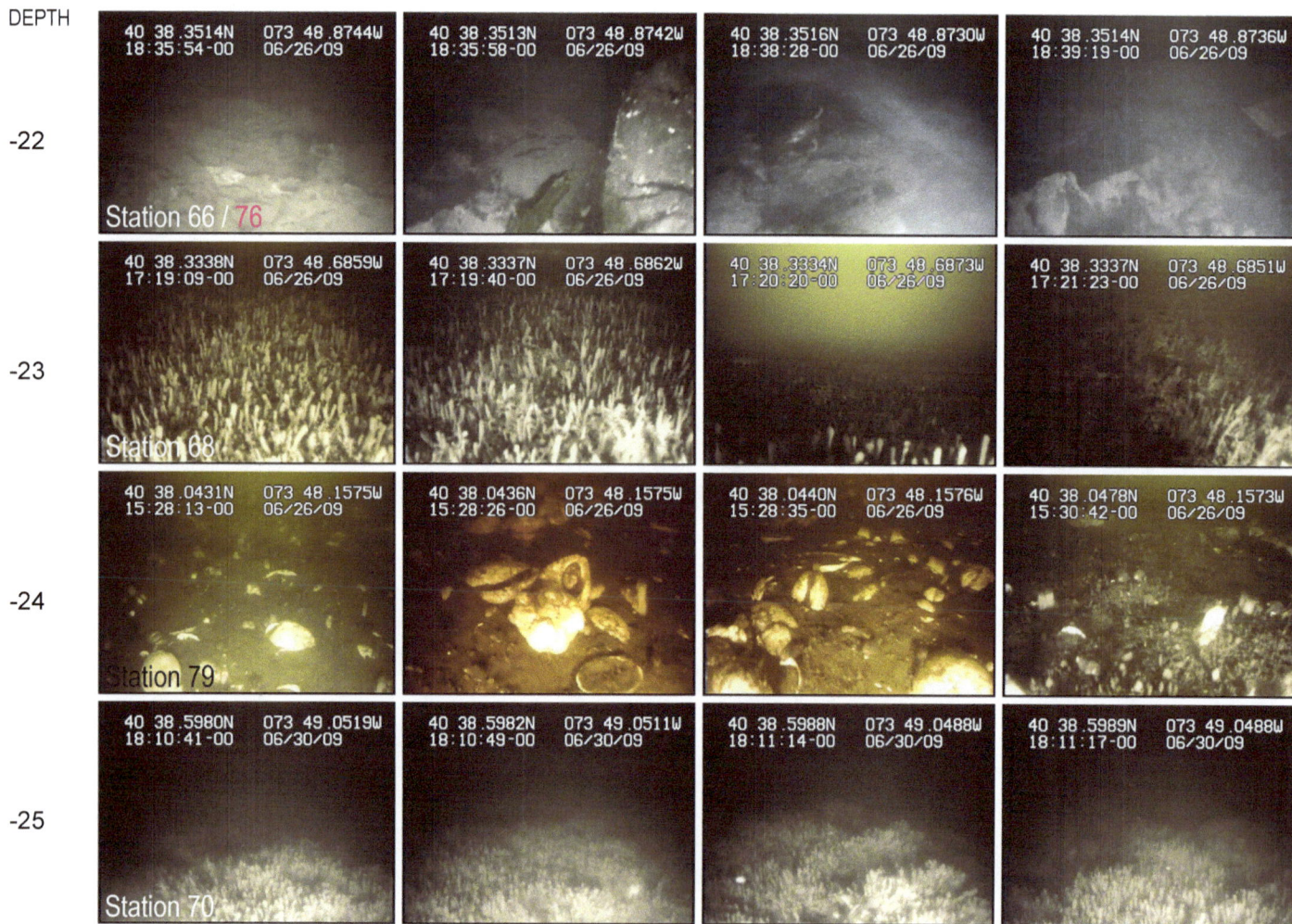

DEPTH

-22

40 38.3514N    073 48.8744W
18:35:54-00    06/26/09
Station 66 / 76

40 38.3513N    073 48.8742W
18:35:58-00    06/26/09

40 38.3516N    073 48.8730W
18:38:28-00    06/26/09

40 38.3514N    073 48.8736W
18:39:19-00    06/26/09

-23

40 38.3338N    073 48.6859W
17:19:09-00    06/26/09
Station 68

40 38.3337N    073 48.6862W
17:19:40-00    06/26/09

40 38.3334N    073 48.6873W
17:20:20-00    06/26/09

40 38.3337N    073 48.6851W
17:21:23-00    06/26/09

-24

40 38.0431N    073 48.1575W
15:28:13-00    06/26/09
Station 79

40 38.0436N    073 48.1575W
15:28:26-00    06/26/09

40 38.0440N    073 48.1576W
15:28:35-00    06/26/09

40 38.0478N    073 48.1573W
15:30:42-00    06/26/09

-25

40 38.5980N    073 49.0519W
18:10:41-00    06/30/09
Station 70

40 38.5982N    073 49.0511W
18:10:49-00    06/30/09

40 38.5988N    073 49.0488W
18:11:14-00    06/30/09

40 38.5989N    073 49.0488W
18:11:17-00    06/30/09

DEPTH

-32

-34

-35

-37

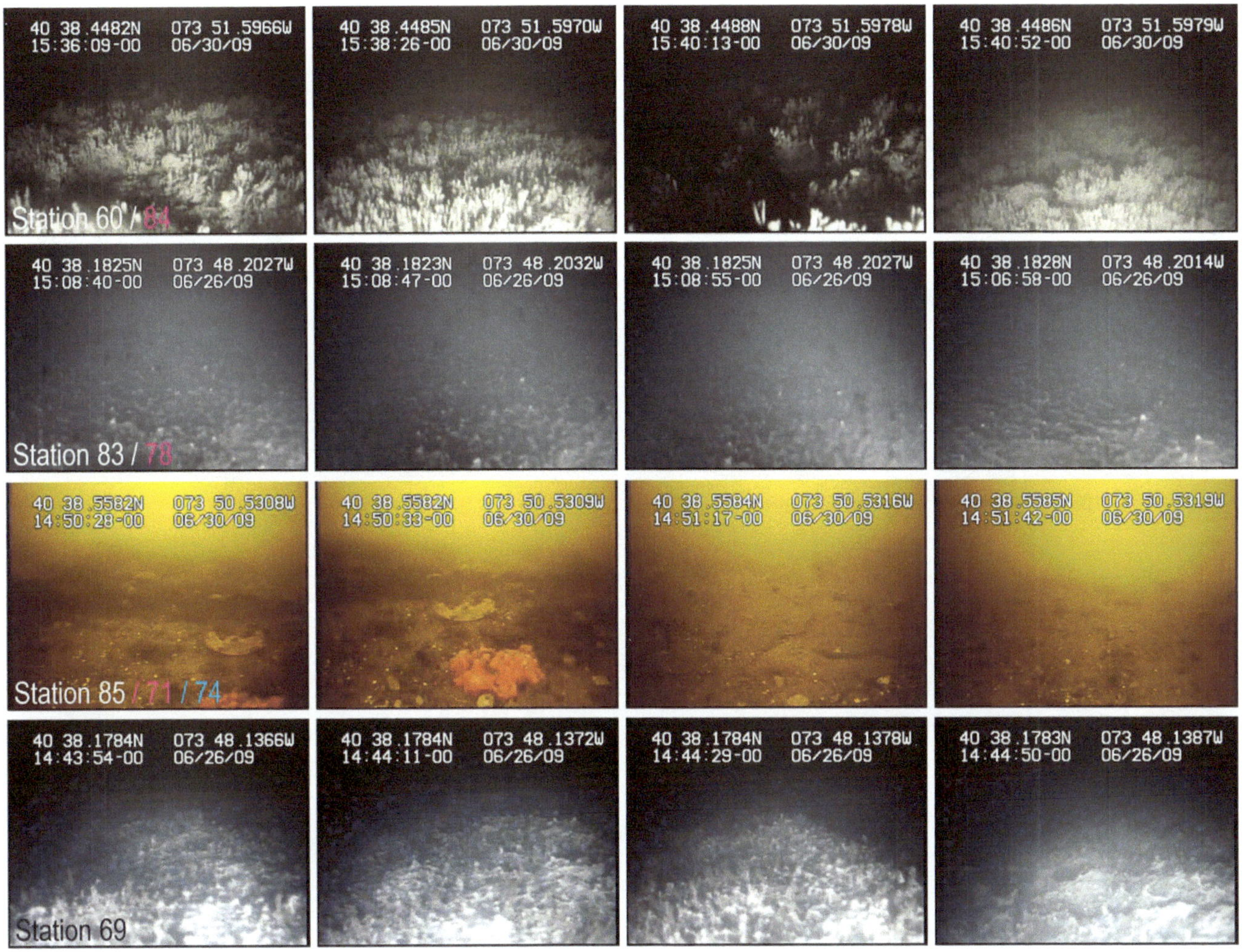

40 34.2206N 073 55.5300W
19:03:40-00 06/17/09

Station 01

40 34.3844N    073 55.5642W
19:23:58-00    06/17/09

Station 03

40 34.3861N     073 55.5639W
19:25:09-00     06/17/09

Station 03

40 34.3835N    073 55.5659W
19:26:20-00    06/17/09

Station 03

40 34.3841N    073 55.5654W
19:26:44-00    06/17/09

Station 03

40 34.6246N    073 51.9900W
19:43:49-00    06/30/09

Station 86

40 34.4302N    073 54.3449W
16:38:45-00    06/19/09

Station 14

40 38.4485N    073 51.5970W
15:38:26-00    06/30/09

Station 60

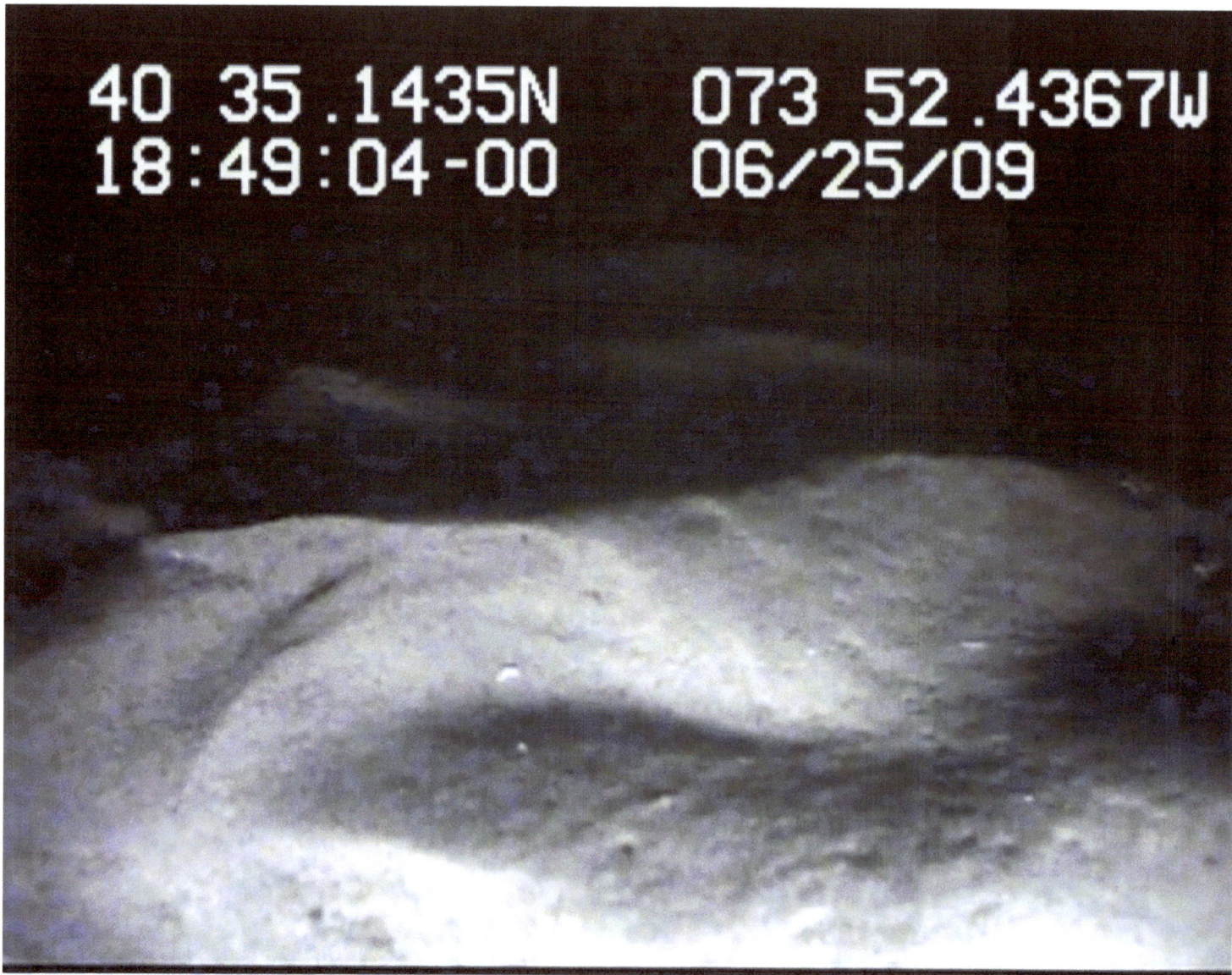

40 35.1435N    073 52.4367W
18:49:04-00    06/25/09

Station 57

## The Bottom of Jamaica Bay

Imagery and data courtesy of U.S. National Park Service, Gateway National Recreation Area. Data collection by Professor Roger D. Flood, School of Marine and Atmospheric Sciences, Stonybrook University, under contract to the National Park Service, as part of the mapping and sampling project "High-Resolution Bathymetric and Backscatter Mapping in Jamaica Bay," completed December 2011. A multi-beam echosounder system and a side-scan sonar system were used for bathymetric mapping in the deep water navigation channels of Jamaica Bay in August and September 2008. The sea bed was photographed at 86 locations in June 2009 with a Deep Blue underwater video camera from Ocean Systems, Inc., and illuminated by small lights when sunlight did not provide sufficient illumination. A full report is available here: https://irma.nps.gov/App/Reference/Profile/2211007

www.ingramcontent.com/pod-product-compliance
Lightning Source LLC
Chambersburg PA
CBHW060826270326
41931CB00002B/73